Grade **4**

Scott Foresman

Classroom Management Handbook for Differentiated Instruction Practice Stations

Glenview, Illinois • Boston, Massachusetts • Chandler, Arizona • Upper Saddle River, New Jersey

ISBN-13: 978-328-47770-8
ISBN-10: 328-47770-2
3 4 5 6 7 8 9 10 VON4 14 13 12 11

Grade 4

Table of Contents

Welcome to Station Time!

Practice Stations Kit

The Leveled Practice Stations Kit helps simplify the task of managing stations by providing ideas for setting up classroom stations, weekly activities for each station, and suggested materials for each station.

Classroom Management Handbook for Differentiated Instruction Practice Stations

The Management Handbook provides valuable resources to help you set up practice stations and to provide differentiated practice that enables you to address students at their instructional levels while they are working independently. The Scott Foresman Differentiated Instruction Practice Stations help students develop as independent thinkers who take responsibility for their own learning. The Handbook provides a suggested classroom floor plan that can be adjusted to fit the particular needs of your classroom. An overview for each station provides suggestions for setting up the stations and essential materials to include. The reproducible Student Work Plans list tasks that students will complete at each station and help students plan and track their assignments at each station.

Practice Station Flip Charts

The Practice Stations Flip Charts are tabletop-sized flip charts with the Practice Stations activities from the Teacher's Edition. Each flip-chart page provides the weekly leveled activities for that station. The activities provide opportunities for students to practice skills and to expand knowledge of the weekly concept. There are six flip charts, one for each station.

- Word Wise (spelling station)
- Word Work (phonics station)
- Works to Know (vocabulary station)

- Let's Write! (writing station)
- Read for Meaning (comprehension station)
- Get Fluent (fluency station)

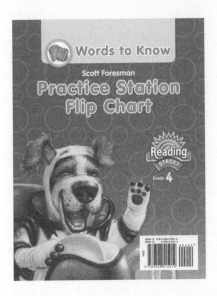

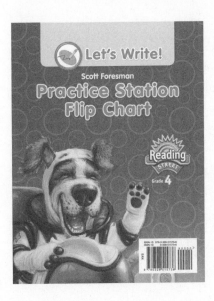

Setting Up the Stations

The classroom environment is an important factor in students' learning. To help create a comfortable environment that is conducive to learning, create separate spaces for the different types of instruction and activities that take place each day.

A Station-Friendly Classroom

As much as possible, a classroom environment should be warm, inviting, and conducive to effective learning for you and your students. As an integral part of that environment, cross-curricular stations should be comfortable areas in which students can work independently, in pairs, or in small groups. To that end, consider some or all of the following suggestions when developing your stations.

- Set aside an area for whole-class instruction and a space for you to work with small groups.
- Think about the function of each station and where it is most appropriately located in the room.
- Provide as much space as possible between noisy and quiet areas.
- Develop traffic patterns that allow for easy movement through and around stations.

One possible classroom setup is shown to the right.

Establish Stations Routines

Station time will be most effective if you develop routines and set clear expectations for students working in the stations. The goal is to enable students to work independently. Following are suggestions to help students reach independence.

- At the beginning of the year, model how to use the stations and coach students on how to be responsible when working in the stations.
- Establish rules for each station, discuss these with students, and post them in the stations.
- Make sure that students understand what is expected of them for each station activity. Post suggestions for early finishers in each station.
- Support students in making their own decisions about what to do at a station and how to solve problems.
- Use a management chart so that students will know where they should be on a daily basis.
- Appoint a "stations monitor" each week whose job it is to update the management chart and make sure that students know where they should be working.
- Distribute copies of "My Work Plan" each week to help students plan their time and tasks.
- Stock each station with appropriate supplies.

Once students are using the stations, you can rotate among them, answering questions, providing direction, guiding research, and assessing performance.

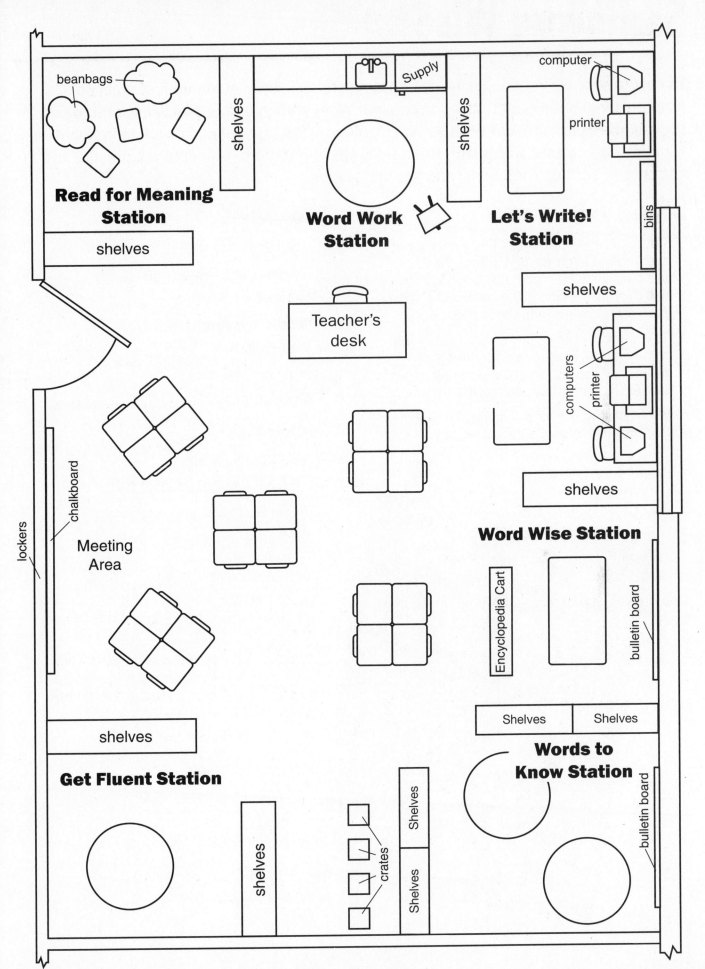

beanbags

Read for Meaning Station

shelves

Word Work Station

Supply

shelves

computer

printer

Let's Write! Station

bins

shelves

Teacher's desk

computers

printer

chalkboard

lockers

Meeting Area

shelves

Word Wise Station

Encyclopedia Cart

bulletin board

Shelves   Shelves

shelves

Get Fluent Station

Words to Know Station

Shelves

crates

Shelves

bulletin board

Word Wise

To ensure success in the phonics and spelling stations, have students first practice word building and pronunciation in the Word Work station before practicing writing and spelling words in the Word Wise station. At Word Wise, students can work individually or with partners to spell words with the weekly spelling pattern. Students will practice the patterns by sorting, combining, and spelling words.

Setting Up the Station

- Students can create a spelling pattern and rule book to keep at the stations. Each week, students can add a page about the skill they just learned. The book will also act as a reference guide in the station.

- As you review the work students are doing in the station, look to see whether they are demonstrating an understanding of previously learned spelling skills.

- To review and practice spelling skills, allow students to use available technology.

Materials

- *Word Wise* Flip Chart
- Teacher-made word cards
- Paper
- Pencils and pens
- Note cards
- Graphic organizers
- Dictionaries

Technology

- Online Dictionary
- Interactive Sound-Spelling Cards
- Online Graphic Organizers

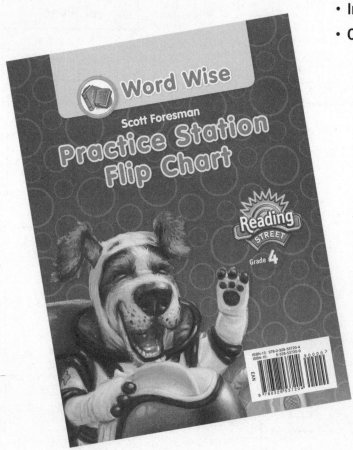

Word Work

At Word Work students can work individually or with partners to identify, build, and pronounce words to practice the phonics and spelling skill. Once students demonstrate an understanding of the skill, they are ready to move to Word Wise to practice spelling and writing words with the same spelling skill.

Setting Up the Station

Provide a table or group of desks where students can work individually and in pairs.

- Students can create a pronunciation chart or book to keep at the station. Each week, students can add a page about the skill they just learned. The book will also act as a reference guide in the station.

- As time allows, listen to see that students are building and pronouncing new and learned words correctly. Model correct pronunciation as needed.

- To review and practice spelling skills, allow students to use available technology.

- Allow students to listen to the Modeled Pronunciation Audio CD for additional practice with letter-sound relationships.

Materials

- *Word Work* Flip Chart

- Teacher-made word cards

- Paper

- Pencils and pens

- Note cards

Technology

- Modeled Pronunciation Audio CD

- Online Graphic Organizers

Words to Know

At Words to Know, the vocabulary station, students will use the lesson vocabulary strategies and word analysis skills to extend and enrich their understanding of key concepts and themes. Students will also build their speaking and reading vocabularies.

Setting Up the Station

Provide a table or group of desks where students can work individually or in pairs.

- Supplement the station with additional vocabulary-building activities that are language-rich.
- Use lesson vocabulary and weekly spelling words with these activities to practice strategies and reinforce understanding of word meanings.

Materials

- *Words to Know* Flip Chart
- Teacher-made word cards
- Paper
- Pencils, pens
- Dictionaries, thesauruses

Technology

- Envision It! Pictured Vocabulary Cards
- Online Dictionary
- Vocabulary Activities

TEACHER TIP

- Make a list of options for early finishers and post them on the board or on an overheard transparency.

- Make a "lost" jar/box so that students will know where to put stray items. These items can then be easily returned to the correct station.

Let's Write!

Let's Write!, the writing station, allows students to work on a variety of writing activities. These activities provide opportunities for students to extend concepts learned while writing in multiple genres.

Setting Up the Station

The writing station may need more space than other stations.

- Designate a table for students who are working on prewriting and drafting activities, and another for revising, editing, and publishing.

- Set up computers for word processing on another table or on a group of desks.

- Stock the station with any necessary writing materials. Include the weekly list of spelling words, vocabulary words, and the Amazing Words to provide practice.

Materials

- *Let's Write!* Flip Chart
- Paper
- Pencils, pens
- Dictionaries, thesauruses
- Graphic organizers
- Revising and editing checklists

Technology

- Online Graphic Organizers
- Online Journal
- Grammar Jammer
- Online Dictionary

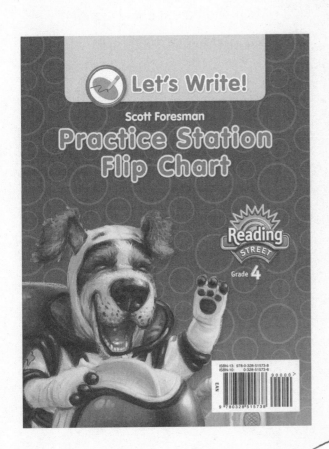

Read for Meaning

At Read for Meaning, the reading comprehension station, students can read additional materials to practice target comprehension skills and strategies. They can also make connections across texts, explore personal interests, or find out more about topics, authors, and genres that are related to the week's concept.

Setting Up the Station

Find a comfortable space for this station away from the main activity of the classroom.

- Include a table and chairs as well as rocking chairs, carpet squares, or beanbags.
- Use shelves, wire rack bins, or plastic tote trays to create an organized classroom library.
- Group books by theme, topic, genre, reading level, or author.

Materials

- *Read for Meaning* Flip Chart
- Leveled Readers
- Paper
- Pencils, pens
- Graphic organizers

Technology

- Leveled Reader Database
- Reading Street Leveled Readers CD-ROM
- Envision It! Animations
- Main and Paired eSelections
- Online Graphic Organizers

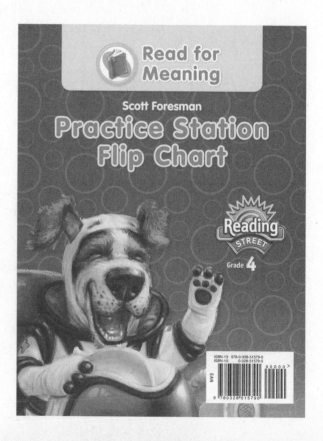

Read for Meaning

Scott Foresman
Practice Station
Flip Chart

Reading STREET

Grade 4

ISBN-13: 978-0-328-51579-0
ISBN-10: 0-328-51579-5

Get Fluent

Get Fluent, the fluency station, is the place where students practice fluent reading. Students will listen to and read aloud various texts while focusing on reading with accuracy, at an appropriate rate, with appropriate phrasing, and with expression and intonation.

Setting Up the Station

Students will often read with a partner. Set up this station where the student work will be the least disruptive to other classmates.

- Locate the station near a computer so students can utilize available technology.

- Provide headsets so that students listening to audio will not be distracted by other noises.

- Arrange the table and chairs to allow partners to work together easily.

- Occasionally reassign partners in order to provide students with a variety of fluency models and partner feedback.

Materials

- *Get Fluent* Flip Chart
- Leveled Readers
- CD player

Technology

- Leveled Reader Database
- Reading Street Leveled Readers CD-ROM
- AudioText CD

ELL-Accessible Stations

The *Scott Foresman Practice Stations* can be adapted to be more accessible to English language learners. Frontloading suggestions and background building information found in the core lesson help support all of the independent activities in the stations. Modeling with picture cues, real objects, and role-playing can help English language learners understand what they need to do without solely depending on language. Students should be encouraged to listen, speak, read, and write during their time in each station. Enhance language production by structuring cooperative learning opportunities at the Practice Stations. Pair students who share the same home language, or have more proficient students work with newcomers. This extra support provides a positive example and support for completing activities in the stations. The stations provide an environment where students can feel comfortable practicing English without worrying about errors they may make.

Word Wise and Word Work

Word Wise and Word Work, the spelling and phonics stations, practice the same set of skills each week, so the stations can be adapted in similar ways. Encourage students to decode the words aloud with a partner. Use the following suggestions to adapt the spelling and phonics stations for English language learners.

- Be sure that students understand the meanings of all of the words before they use the station.

- When possible, introduce any cognates or language transfer skills that will help students better understand the words practiced.

- Review the spelling words or spelling patterns using the Sound-Spelling Charts.

- Use one of the teacher-made word cards to model decoding the spelling pattern.

- Point to the spellings of the word as you say each sound. Model blending each word.

- Have groups of mixed abilities use letter tiles to spell out the spelling words. Students should read the words they made to the other groups of students. Offer guidance as necessary.

Words to Know

English language learners can benefit in Words to Know by using visuals and real objects to scaffold meaning. Encourage students to use their home languages to transfer any knowledge or strategies to what they are practicing. The following suggestions can be used to adapt the vocabulary station.

- Introduce any cognates or language transfer skills that will help students better understand the lesson vocabulary.
- Revisit the lesson vocabulary words with students daily. Help students say each word and encourage oral production.
- Review any suffixes, prefixes, word endings, or word origins students may encounter in the weekly lesson vocabulary.
- Have groups of mixed abilities work together using letter tiles to spell their lesson vocabulary words. Have more advanced students model and define the words.

Let's Write!

Students at all proficiency levels should be given a variety of materials they need to be able to write successfully. Some students may benefit from brainstorming and using graphic organizers while some may benefit by working independently with a writing prompt. The adaptations below may help your English language learners succeed in the writing station.

- Provide sentence frames, writing prompts, or writing models to assist students' writing.
- For beginning and intermediate students, write out sentences they dictate. Allow them to copy the sentences and then read them aloud to you.
- More advanced students can write sentences and share with a partner.

Read for Meaning

Have a variety of ELL and ELD Readers available at Read for Meaning. Students may benefit from reviewing the comprehension skill with the Envision It! illustrations in the Student Edition or the Picture It! blackline masters found in the *English Language Learner's Handbook.* The station may be adapted using the following suggestions.

- When possible, use picture cues to review the comprehension skill.
- Choose a selection that is appropriate to students' reading level. Read aloud the selection with the students.
- During reading, ask questions or fill out a graphic organizer with students to monitor their comprehension.
- Allow beginning and intermediate students to orally explain the relationships between the comprehension skill and the selection read. More advanced students can complete this activity by writing sentences.

Get Fluent

Guide students to determine the best fluency routine for them to use at this station. Be sure all students are practicing the different fluency traits with texts at their level and that they understand what they are reading. Adapt the fluency station using the following suggestions.

- Have pairs of mixed-ability students reread the ELL or ELD Reader to each other.
- Circulate and evaluate intermediate to advanced students for word recognition, accuracy, and prosody.
- Work individually with beginning and intermediate students, focusing on decoding for meaning. Provide support as needed.

The Practice Stations provide valuable opportunities for students to gain knowledge and increase their confidence, thereby making their social and academic classroom experiences more meaningful. In addition, students' involvement in the stations will strengthen their performance in all areas of instruction, and their work in the stations will positively affect their ability to function as active and independent learners.

Assessment

Station activities provide excellent opportunities for informal, ongoing assessments that are useful in guiding instruction. Effective station activities provide opportunities for students to engage in meaningful tasks that advance learning in all areas, especially reading and writing. Emphasize to students that activities completed in the stations are important and will be assessed. Use information gathered from these assessments to guide instruction for individuals, groups, or the entire class.

Assessment Suggestions

Observe Student Work

- Determine what you expect in terms of student behaviors and attitudes and develop checklists based on those expectations.

- Focus on one or more students each day and keep informal notes about behavior, motivation, performance, or any other information you think is significant.

- Document students' learning and work habits and record social interactions.

- Hold periodic, structured conferences with students about their work.

- Plan support that addresses a student's particular strength or need.

- Record any information that will help make instructional decisions. You may want to use the Observation Record on page 17.

Create and Post Rubrics

- Create a rubric to assess how well students follow station directions.

- Use a rubric to assess student creativity and motivation.

- Post a rubric in Let's Write!, the writing station, so that students are aware of assessment criteria for writing projects.

Establish Portfolios

- Help students establish portfolios for station activities in progress.

- Use portfolio contents as a measure of progress and growth over time.

Involve Students in Self-Assessments

- Have students evaluate their own work and set goals for improvement.

- Have students evaluate each other's work in pairs and groups.

Observation Record

Date.......................... Student...

Date.......................... Student...

Date.......................... Student...

Date.......................... Student...

Date.......................... Student...

Date.......................... Student...

Student Work Plans

What Are Student Work Plans?

Pages 19–48 contain lesson-specific reproducible work plans for students to use during their independent activity time. Each work plan lists the tasks that students will complete, in stations or independently, while you meet with small groups. The work plans help students remember their assignments, plan their time, and keep track of what they've done. Work plans allow students to take responsibility and will aid them in becoming successful independent learners.

How Do I Use the Student Work Plans?

Begin by explaining the activities in the Practice Stations to students. Then distribute copies of *My Work Plan* and review the tasks. Be sure students understand that they will check the box next to each task as they complete it. Remind students that if they finish an activity before time is up, they should answer the Wrap Up Your Week questions or read silently. At the end of the week, you can collect students' work plans, or you can send them home.

If you prefer, you can customize a work plan for one or more students or for use during a particular lesson. For this purpose, a generic work plan can be found on p. 49.

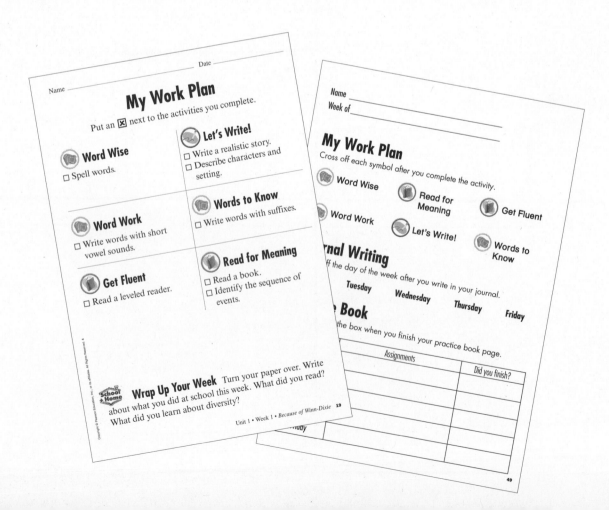

My Work Plan

Put an ☒ next to the activities you complete.

 ## Word Wise

☐ Spell words.

 ## Let's Write!

☐ Write a realistic story.
☐ Describe characters and setting.

 ## Word Work

☐ Write words with short vowel sounds.

 ## Words to Know

☐ Write words with suffixes.

 ## Get Fluent

☐ Read a leveled reader.

 ## Read for Meaning

☐ Read a book.
☐ Identify the sequence of events.

Wrap Up Your Week Turn your paper over. Write about what you did at school this week. What did you read? What did you learn about diversity?

Name _____ Date _____

My Work Plan

Put an ☒ next to the activities you complete.

 Word Wise

☐ Spell words.

 Let's Write!

☐ Study the Words to Know.
☐ Make a word game.

 Word Work

☐ Write words with short vowel sounds.

 Words to Know

☐ Write words with suffixes.

 Get Fluent

☐ Read a leveled reader.

 Read for Meaning

☐ Read a book.
☐ Identify a sequence of events.

School + Home **Wrap Up Your Week** Turn your paper over. Write about what you did at school this week. What did you read? What did you learn about opportunities in new places?

My Work Plan

Put an ☒ next to the activities you complete.

 ## Word Wise

☐ Circle letters that spell long vowel sounds.
☐ Write sentences.

 ## Let's Write!

☐ Write a composition about a job.

 ## Word Work

☐ Sort words into columns.

 ## Words to Know

☐ Define words with endings.
☐ Write sentences.

 ## Get Fluent

☐ Read a leveled reader.

 ## Read for Meaning

☐ Write about the author's purpose.

School + Home **Wrap Up Your Week** Turn your paper over. Write about what you did at school this week. What did you read? What did you learn about exploring new places?

Name _____   Date _____

My Work Plan

Put an ☒ next to the activities you complete.

 Word Wise

☐ Write sentences.
☐ List words.

 Let's Write!

☐ Write a parody with a partner.

 Word Work

☐ Circle long vowel sounds.
☐ Write rhyming words.
☐ Write a poem.

 Words to Know

☐ Define multiple-meaning words.
☐ Write sentences.

 Get Fluent

☐ Read a leveled reader.

 Read for Meaning

☐ Write about plot, characters, and setting.

Wrap Up Your Week Turn your paper over. Write about what you did at school this week. What did you read? What did you learn about the Southwest.

Name _____ Date _____

My Work Plan

Put an ⊠ next to the activities you complete.

 ## Word Wise

☐ Circle letters that spell long e.
☐ Write sentences.
☐ List words.

 ## Let's Write!

☐ Write a friendly letter.

 ## Word Work

☐ Fill out a chart.

 ## Words to Know

☐ Write synonyms and antonyms.
☐ Write sentences.

 ## Get Fluent

☐ Read a leveled reader.

 ## Read for Meaning

☐ Write about the author's purpose.

Wrap Up Your Week Turn your paper over. Write about what you did at school this week. What did you read? What did you learn about the West?

Name _____ Date _____

My Work Plan

Put an ☒ next to the activities you complete.

 ## Word Wise

☐ Write sentences.
☐ List words.

 ## Let's Write!

☐ Write a personal narrative.

 ## Word Work

☐ Circle letters that spell long *u*.
☐ Write rhyming words.

 ## Words to Know

☐ Circle base words.
☐ Write sentences.

 ## Get Fluent

☐ Read a leveled reader.

 ## Read for Meaning

☐ Write about the main idea and details.

Wrap Up Your Week Turn your paper over. Write about what you did at school this week. What did you read? What did you learn about developing new understandings?

Name _____ Date _____

My Work Plan

Put an ☒ next to the activities you complete.

 ## Word Wise

☐ Circle letters that make a plural.
☐ Write sentences.

 ## Let's Write!

☐ Write a limerick.
☐ Proofread the rhyme scheme.

 ## Word Work

☐ Write the singular form.
☐ List words.

 ## Words to Know

☐ Circle base words.
☐ Write sentences.

 ## Get Fluent

☐ Read a leveled reader.

 ## Read for Meaning

☐ Write about causes and effects.

Wrap Up Your Week Turn your paper over. Write about what you did at school this week. What did you read? What did you learn about working together?

Name _____   Date _____

My Work Plan

Put an ☒ next to the activities you complete.

 Word Wise

☐ Circle letters that make a plural.
☐ Write sentences.

 Let's Write!

☐ Write a news article.

 Word Work

☐ Write the singular form.
☐ List plurals.

 Words to Know

☐ Define unknown words.
☐ List the parts of speech.
☐ Write sentences.

 Get Fluent

☐ Read a leveled reader.

 Read for Meaning

☐ Draw a conclusion.
☐ Use supporting details.

Wrap Up Your Week Turn your paper over. Write about what you did at school this week. What did you read? What did you learn about team accomplishments?

Name _____ Date _____

My Work Plan

Put an ☒ next to the activities you complete.

 ## Word Wise

☐ Write sentences.
☐ List words.
☐ Write a paragraph.

 ## Let's Write!

☐ Write a poem.
☐ Use similes or examples of assonance.

 ## Word Work

☐ Sort words into a chart.
☐ Say words.

 ## Words to Know

☐ Circle base words.
☐ Write sentences.

Get Fluent

☐ Read along with a partner.

 ## Read for Meaning

☐ Draw a conclusion.
☐ Use supporting details.

 Wrap Up Your Week Turn your paper over. Write about what you did at school this week. What did you read? What did you learn about how people and animals work together as a team?

Name _____ Date _____

My Work Plan

Put an ☒ next to the activities you complete.

 ## Word Wise

☐ List words.
☐ Circle consonant pairs.
☐ Write sentences.

 ## Let's Write!

☐ Write directions.
☐ Number steps.

 ## Word Work

☐ Circle consonant pairs.
☐ Say words.
☐ List words.

 ## Words to Know

☐ Define unknown words.
☐ List parts of speech.
☐ Write sentences.

 ## Get Fluent

☐ Read along with a partner.

 ## Read for Meaning

☐ Write statements of fact and opinion.
☐ Use supporting details.

School + Home **Wrap Up Your Week** Turn your paper over. Write about what you did at school this week. What did you read? What did you learn about the President's job?

28 Unit 2 • Week 5 • *So You Want to Be President?*

My Work Plan

Put an ☒ next to the activities you complete.

 Word Wise

☐ List words.
☐ Write sentences.

 Let's Write!

☐ Write a persuasive article.

 Word Work

☐ Sort words into columns.

 Words to Know

☐ Define unknown words.
☐ List parts of speech.
☐ Write sentences.

 Get Fluent

☐ Read a leveled reader.

 Read for Meaning

☐ Write the main idea and details.

School + Home Wrap Up Your Week Turn your paper over. Write about what you did at school this week. What did you read? What did you learn about patterns in nature?

Name _____ Date _____

My Work Plan

Put an ☒ next to the activities you complete.

 Word Wise

☐ Circle base words.
☐ Write sentences.

 Let's Write!

☐ Write a narrative poem.
☐ Proofread for rhythm.

 Word Work

☐ Fill out a chart.

 Words to Know

☐ Define multiple-meaning words.
☐ Write sentences.

 Get Fluent

☐ Read a leveled reader.

 Read for Meaning

☐ Write about graphic sources.

Wrap Up Your Week Turn your paper over. Write about what you did at school this week. What did you read? What did you learn about animal migration?

Name _____   Date _____

My Work Plan

Put an ☒ next to the activities you complete.

 ## Word Wise

☐ List homophones.
☐ Write sentences.

 ## Let's Write!

☐ Write and illustrate an invitation.

 ## Word Work

☐ List homophones.

 ## Words to Know

☐ Define multiple-meaning words.
☐ Write sentences.

 ## Get Fluent

☐ Read a leveled reader.

 ## Read for Meaning

☐ Write facts and opinions.

Wrap Up Your Week Turn your paper over. Write about what you did at school this week. What did you read? What did you learn about day and night?

Name _____ Date _____

My Work Plan

Put an ☒ next to the activities you complete.

 Word Wise

☐ List homophones.
☐ Write sentences.

 Let's Write!

☐ Write a myth.
☐ Use a variety of sentences.

 Word Work

☐ Sort words in a chart.
☐ Write rhyming words.

 Words to Know

☐ Use context clues to define unfamiliar words.
☐ Write sentences.

 Get Fluent

☐ Read a leveled reader.

 Read for Meaning

☐ Make a generalization.
☐ Use supporting details.

Wrap Up Your Week Turn your paper over. Write about what you did at school this week. What did you read? What did you learn about storms?

My Work Plan

Put an ☒ next to the activities you complete.

 ## Word Wise

☐ Circle words in compound words.
☐ Write sentences.

 ## Let's Write!

☐ Write a formal letter.

 ## Word Work

☐ Divide compound words.
☐ List compound words.
☐ Write rhyming words.

 ## Words to Know

☐ Define root words.
☐ List words that share roots.
☐ Write sentences.

 ## Get Fluent

☐ Read a leveled reader.

 ## Read for Meaning

☐ Write causes and effects.

Wrap Up Your Week Turn your paper over. Write about what you did at school this week. What did you read? What did you learn about changes in nature?

Name _____ Date _____

My Work Plan

Put an ☒ next to the activities you complete.

 ## Word Wise

☐ Circle the possessive.
☐ Write sentences.
☐ List base words.

 ## Let's Write!

☐ Write a book summary.

 ## Word Work

☐ List words.
☐ Identify words as singular or plural.

 ## Words to Know

☐ Circle suffixes.
☐ Write sentences.

 ## Get Fluent

☐ Read a leveled reader.

 ## Read for Meaning

☐ Make a generalization.
☐ Use supporting details.

School + Home ## Wrap Up Your Week
Turn your paper over. Write about what you did at school this week. What did you read? What did you learn about perception?

Name _____ Date _____

My Work Plan

Put an ☒ next to the activities you complete.

 ## Word Wise

☐ Write sentences.
☐ List words that form contractions.

 ## Let's Write!

☐ Write a mystery.

 ## Word Work

☐ List contractions.

 ## Words to Know

☐ Write synonyms and antonyms.

 ## Get Fluent

☐ Read a leveled reader.

 ## Read for Meaning

☐ Compare and contrast characters.

'School' + Home **Wrap Up Your Week** Turn your paper over. Write about what you did at school this week. What did you read? What did you learn about animal behavior?

My Work Plan

Put an ☒ next to the activities you complete.

 ## Word Wise

☐ Circle final syllables.
☐ Write sentences.
☐ List words.

 ## Let's Write!

☐ Write a song.
☐ List rhyming words.

 ## Word Work

☐ Group words by final syllable.
☐ Write rhyming words.
☐ Write a poem.

 ## Words to Know

☐ Define multiple-meaning words.
☐ Write sentences.

 ## Get Fluent

☐ Read a leveled reader.

 ## Read for Meaning

☐ Compare and contrast settings.

School + Home ## Wrap Up Your Week Turn your paper over. Write about what you did at school this week. What did you read? What did you learn about why secret codes are necessary?

Name _____ Date _____

My Work Plan

Put an ☒ next to the activities you complete.

 Word Wise

☐ List words.
☐ Write sentences.

 Let's Write!

☐ Write step-by-step instructions.

 Word Work

☐ Sort words in a chart.

 Words to Know

☐ Define unknown words.
☐ Write sentences.

 Get Fluent

☐ Read a leveled reader.

 Read for Meaning

☐ Write the sequence of events.

Wrap Up Your Week Turn your paper over. Write about what you did at school this week. What did you read? What did you learn about communication?

My Work Plan

Put an ☒ next to the activities you complete.

 Word Wise

☐ List words.
☐ Write sentences.

 Let's Write!

☐ Write a problem-solution essay.

 Word Work

☐ Circle letters that spell /j/, /ks/, and /kw/ sounds.
☐ List words.

 Words to Know

☐ Circle Greek or Latin roots.
☐ Write sentences.

 Get Fluent

☐ Read a leveled reader.

 Read for Meaning

☐ Write about graphic sources.

Wrap Up Your Week Turn your paper over. Write about what you did at school this week. What did you read? What did you learn about inquiry?

My Work Plan

Put an ☒ next to the activities you complete.

 ## Word Wise

☐ Write sentences.
☐ List words with prefixes.

 ## Let's Write!

☐ Write an adventure story.

 ## Word Work

☐ Circle base words.

 ## Words to Know

☐ Write synonyms and antonyms.
☐ Write sentences.

 ## Get Fluent

☐ Read a leveled reader.

 ## Read for Meaning

☐ Write about characters and plot.

School + Home **Wrap Up Your Week** Turn your paper over. Write about what you did at school this week. What did you read? What did you learn about preparing for emergencies?

Name _____ Date _____

My Work Plan

Put an ☒ next to the activities you complete.

 Word Wise

☐ List multisyllabic words.
☐ List numbers of syllables.

 Let's Write!

☐ Write a fantasy.

 Word Work

☐ List multisyllabic words.

 Words to Know

☐ Define homographs.
☐ Write sentences.

 Get Fluent

☐ Read a leveled reader.

 Read for Meaning

☐ Write the author's purpose.
☐ Use supporting details.

Wrap Up Your Week Turn your paper over. Write about what you did at school this week. What did you read? What did you learn about ancient civilizations?

My Work Plan

Put an ☒ next to the activities you complete.

 ## Word Wise

☐ List words with double-consonant.

☐ Write a poem.

 ## Let's Write!

☐ Write a legend.

 ## Word Work

☐ Circle words with double consonants.

☐ Write sentences.

 ## Words to Know

☐ Circle Greek or Latin roots.

☐ Write sentences.

 ## Get Fluent

☐ Read a leveled reader.

 ## Read for Meaning

☐ Compare and contrast two settings.

School + Home **Wrap Up Your Week** Turn your paper over. Write about what you did at school this week. What did you read? What did you learn about space explorations?

My Work Plan

Put an ☒ next to the activities you complete.

 Word Wise

☐ Circle Greek word parts.
☐ Write sentences.
☐ List words.

 Let's Write!

☐ Write a thank-you note.

 Word Work

☐ Sort words into a chart.

 Words to Know

☐ Use contact clues to define unfamiliar words.
☐ Write sentences.

 Get Fluent

☐ Read a leveled reader.

 Read for Meaning

☐ Write about the characters, plot, and theme.

School + Home **Wrap Up Your Week** Turn your paper over. Write about what you did at school this week. What did you read? What did you learn about adaptations in harsh climates?

Name _____ Date _____

My Work Plan

Put an ☒ next to the activities you complete.

 ## Word Wise

☐ Circle Greek or Latin word parts.
☐ Write sentences.
☐ List words.

 ## Let's Write!

☐ Write and illustrate a persuasive ad.

 ## Word Work

☐ Group words by prefixes.

 ## Words to Know

☐ Define words with prefixes.
☐ Write sentences.

 ## Get Fluent

☐ Read a leveled reader.

 ## Read for Meaning

☐ Write about the main idea and details.

Wrap Up Your Week Turn your paper over. Write about what you did at school this week. What did you read? What did you learn about the moon?

My Work Plan

Put an ☒ next to the activities you complete.

 Word Wise

☐ Write sentences.
☐ List related words.

 Let's Write!

☐ Write a personal narrative.

 Word Work

☐ List related words.

 Words to Know

☐ Find synonyms.
☐ Write sentences.

 Get Fluent

☐ Read a leveled reader.

Read for Meaning

☐ Draw a conclusion.
☐ Use supporting details.

School + Home **Wrap Up Your Week** Turn your paper over. Write about what you did at school this week. What did you read? What did you learn about equal opportunities?

My Work Plan

Put an ☒ next to the activities you complete.

 Word Wise

☐ Circle letters that form the schwa sound.
☐ Write sentences.

 Let's Write!

☐ Write a cause-and-effect essay.

 Word Work

☐ List words with the schwa sound.

 Words to Know

☐ Define root words.
☐ Write sentences.
☐ List words.

 Get Fluent

☐ Read a leveled reader.

 Read for Meaning

☐ Write about causes and effects.

Wrap Up Your Week Turn your paper over. Write about what you did at school this week. What did you read? What did you learn about challenges?

My Work Plan

Put an ☒ next to the activities you complete.

 ## Word Wise

☐ Circle base words.
☐ Write sentences.

 ## Let's Write!

☐ Write a book review.

 ## Word Work

☐ Write base words.
☐ Write sentences.
☐ List words with prefixes.

 ## Words to Know

☐ Define multiple-meaning words.
☐ Write sentences.

 ## Get Fluent

☐ Read a leveled reader.

 ## Read for Meaning

☐ Write about facts and opinions.

Wrap Up Your Week

Turn your paper over. Write about what you did at school this week. What did you read? What did you learn about coming to a new culture?

Name _____ Date _____

My Work Plan

Put an ☒ next to the activities you complete.

 Word Wise

☐ Circle base words.
☐ Write sentences.

 Let's Write!

☐ Write a skit.
☐ Use dialogue.

 Word Work

☐ Write base words.
☐ Write sentences.
☐ List words with suffixes.

 Words to Know

☐ Use context clues to define unfamiliar words.
☐ Write sentences.

 Get Fluent

☐ Read a leveled reader.

 Read for Meaning

☐ Write the sequence of events.

School + Home **Wrap Up Your Week** Turn your paper over. Write about what you did at school this week. What did you read? What did you learn about sacrifice?

My Work Plan

Put an ☒ next to the activities you complete.

 Word Wise

☐ Circle base words.
☐ Write sentences.

 Let's Write!

☐ Write a play or scene.
☐ Use dialogue.

 Word Work

☐ Write base words.
☐ Write sentences.
☐ List words with suffixes.

 Words to Know

☐ Use context clues to define unfamiliar words.
☐ Write sentences.

 Get Fluent

☐ Read a leveled reader.

 Read for Meaning

☐ Make a generalization.
☐ Use supporting details.

'School + Home' **Wrap Up Your Week** Turn your paper over. Write about what you did at school this week. What did you read? What did you learn about space explorations?

Name _____

Week of _____

My Work Plan

Cross off each symbol after you complete the activity.

 Word Wise   **Read for Meaning**   **Get Fluent**

 Word Work   **Let's Write!**   **Words to Know**

Journal Writing

Cross off the day of the week after you write in your journal.

Monday   **Tuesday**   **Wednesday**   **Thursday**   **Friday**

Practice Book

Draw an X in the box when you finish your practice book page.

	Assignments	Did you finish?
Monday		
Tuesday		
Wednesday		
Thursday		
Friday